Change the World 9 to 5

50 actions to change the world at work

Designed by: Antidote
Written by: Steve Henry
Created by: Tim Ashton, Chris Wigan, Oliver Davies, Sarah Carr and Zoë Bather
Additional ideas by Nicholla Longley and Sophie Lewis
For We Are What We Do: David Robinson, Eugénie Harvey, Nick Walker,
Sara Smith-Laing, Becca Leed and Sandra Deeble

 SHORT BOOKS

we are what we do ©

We Are What We Do is a Community Links project
(registered charity number 1018517). Community Links
tackles the causes and consequences of social exclusion
in east London and shares the local experience with
practitioners and policy makers nationwide.

We believe in acting local and thinking global.

As with our first book, 'Change the World for a Fiver',
everyone who has contributed to 'Change the World 9 to 5'
has done so for free or for the cost of their materials.
More than 65 people in total donated their time and
talents – this includes writers, designers, illustrators,
photographers and researchers. Additionally our publisher,
Short Books, and our distributor, TBS, have donated their
services to the project. We are hugely grateful to them all
as their generosity means we are able to keep the price of
the book so low.

Money raised from the sale of the book will be used
to cover the costs of printing and should there be any
surplus this will be used to develop further We Are What
We Do projects in the UK and all round the world. These
include education materials such as our lesson plan,
grass-roots activity in communities acrosss the UK, a
range of merchandise, international launches and more
books! You can find information about all of these and
about our work in other countries by visiting our website
– www.wearewhatwedo.org

For further information about Community Links,
please visit www.community-links.org

Most of us spend most of our waking lives – working.

And how we feel about it is important.

One way of looking at work is like this. It's a place where quite often people are doing what they want to do or were trained to do – with a group of people they consider good friends.

Similarly, one way of looking at this book is to imagine creating the best possible working environment... the best way to spend our 9 to 5... not just to change the world, but also to make everybody happier.

So, how do we do that?

Going the extra mile is a great start – the bus driver who helps with the buggy, the dinner lady who knows the names of all the children.

Then there are surprising small differences we can all make – if every office worker wasted just one less staple, for instance, we'd save 120 tonnes of steel every year.

This book is full of suggestions and ideas to help you change the world and make the people around you happier.

And you might be surprised by what you can achieve if you set your mind to it.

For instance, 65% of UK business leaders said they would change their policies if pressed by their employees.

We know change is possible, on an unimaginable scale. We published 'Change the World for a Fiver' two years ago and have now sold more than half a million copies worldwide. Thousands of individuals have been developing those first 50 actions in their own way, volunteering lite, making their voices heard, becoming part of something bigger than themselves.

It's all based on a very simple formula:
small changes $\times$ lots of people = BIG change.

And, if making the planet a happier, safer, more sustainable place isn't a good enough target, then there's even a business case. A 2005 poll showed that 82% of us believe it is important to buy from companies who share our concerns.

It all makes sense.

So – imagine, believe and begin.

How to use this book

This is a book of simple, everyday actions which we reckon pretty much all of us can do during the working day. It begins with ACTION 51, picking up where our last book, 'Change the World for a Fiver', left off. The ideas came from hundreds of suggestions we received from people in all walks of life and from all corners of the globe. In addition to the 50 actions in the main body of the book, you'll find 500 more on the reverse of the jacket. We hope you'll read them all and choose which actions suit you and your workplace.

To help you spread the word and get others involved, we've included ACTION 65, Pass this book around, so you can treat this book like a library book. Simply fill in your name and pass it on to another person. When the book has been passed on 20 times (and 20 people have filled in their names) you can send the book back to us (visit www.wearewhatwedo.org for details) and we'll send you a replacement book free of charge (and we'll recycle your old one).

At We Are What We Do we aim to please – you suggested we do a book which could be used at work and we've done one. You suggested the kinds of actions which we should put in it, and we've put them in. So if you think we've missed anything or got anything wrong in this book, please let us know by emailing us at suggestions@wearewhatwedo.org

051

Find out where your lunch has come from

The average kiwi fruit flown in from New Zealand travels 12,000 miles to be part of your lunch.

And, according to the experts, that kiwi fruit creates five times its own weight in greenhouse gases, getting here.

Which might lead you to imagine that the little fruit spent the entire trip farting.

(As quite a lot of people do on planes. And most of them are oblivious to the fact, because they're wearing huge ear-phones.)

But in fact it's just because of the fuel employed in getting the fruit here.

Still... if the image of a farting kiwi fruit makes you think twice about eating stuff flown in out of season, maybe it's a useful one.

Photo: Nick Walker

NEVER THROW PAPER AWAY. THERE IS NO AWAY.

052

Recycle waste paper

There is no 'away' – that is a profound thought. Someone like Chris Martin should turn that line into an album title and before you know it, they'd have a huge hit on their hands and be able to fly away to the Bahamas.

But when it comes to rubbish, there really ISN'T any 'away'.

We think it disappears into thin air, like a dove in a Paul Daniels magic trick.

But it doesn't. It doesn't go to the evil planet Zog or into a little clearing in the woods where Dusty Bin plays leapfrog with Ted Rogers all day long.

It sticks around, for thousands of years.

By the way, in the case of Paul Daniels' disappearing dove, it goes up a hole in Paul's... ah, now that would be telling.

FYI: Every year we need a forest the size of Wales to provide all of the paper we use in Britain.

053

Calculate your carbon footprint

If you visit carbonneutral.com, you can calculate how much carbon you emit while travelling to and from work. Then – on the same site – they'll tell you how you can erase that carbon footprint, easily.

This applies to companies as well as individuals. HSBC was the first bank to go 'carbon neutral' and BSkyB, the first media company. How does that make you feel about those two companies?

Let's face it. We all leave a mess behind us.

The difference is, mature people clear it up afterwards.

I just don't like it.
Yes... but what IS it?
That looks like that thing they tried last year. That didn't work either.

...a seven iron is probably enough on the 13th...

It looks like something my daughter made.

It'll never work...

Why on earth would anyone want that?

054

Don't be an ideas killer

At Unilever they have an approach they call 'Build' – i.e. build on what other people say, don't knock it down. Helpful ways to do this do NOT include the following:

'I think what Brian meant to say is this...'

'Great idea. Unfortunately, when Smallbottles tried it, it bankrupted them...'

Or

'I love it. But what do I know? I'm as mad as a lorry.'

055

Use a biro from start to finish

People throw things away too easily. They throw away their charming childhood illusions. Their talent. Their friendships. Their marriages.

But more important than all these things are their biros. (Well, maybe we're exaggerating a little bit, to make a point.)

A plastic pen in landfill will still be there in 50,000 years. Which is not a lot of use to anybody. Unless you imagine that in 50,000 years' time, the world will be populated by super-intelligent beings who have managed to solve all the problems afflicting the human race. Except that they keep forgetting to bring a biro with them.

FYI: Daily worldwide sales figures of biros exceed 14 million pens.

Yippeee! Yippee! Whoaaa! I looove a n
The first line. A whole life ahead. S
shopping lists, doodles, graphs, n
of arrows. It's supposed to mean som
Sympathy, a poisoned pen lett
Or a confession, killing of a dreadfl.
I think they call them, like Flee e
disapointment like 'freshen and
one but you know what I mean. T
Pretty good eh? I bet there are no
ask me. We should just do away w.
letter 'o' is pointless. I tell you so
a word and it means Russian peas
which for a first move is the high
is quite cool too. Cincinnati is gre
university. Swimming is a good
this: Swimming. Bungalow, doo
biro is good, just nothing special.
the biro now and some of them
though. The original biro — like n
going down the tube, sometimes with
biro has in it? You know di
has nearly a quarter as much as engli
earthquake and then subsides. And when it
have to work out whether your roots have
inconceivable that you should ever part. B
day and really thought it was powerful. This is
were at school and the story you were hunting Help to fill

pen. Like a new cheque book, a new pen is a great thing. ...tences. paragraphs. ~~cross~~ crossings outs, signatures, ...re doodles, I love a good doodle especially arrows, it's ...thing - ambition I think. A letter of thanks, a note of ... perhaps. A love letter. A poem. A note to the milkman ...eed. Deed that's one of those back to front words. Palindrome ...! or face decaf, usually palindromes are a bit of a ...melette frustrated salad - well that isn't actually a prope... ...s _is_ a good one: Marge lets Norah see Sharon's telegram ...lindromes starting with q. Q is a pointless letter if you ... it. I mean a letter that can only exist with another ...etting that isn't pointless 'Muzika' that really is ...ts. It also means 128 points on a scrabble board ...st you can get. Gossamer is a lovely word. Flannel ...t. Not the place, although it does have a cool looking ...ord to write, especially if you write it with italics like ... (again) and zoom are my favourites. In truth this ... can get rollerballs and other clever developments of ...el lovely to write with. This one still feels quite new ...one has the added benefit of seeing the ink ...the air bubbles. I wonder just how many words each new ...rent languages use more letters - German for example ... I think. Love is a temporary madness. It erupts like an ...subsides you have to make a decision. You ...ecome so entwined together that it is ...cause this is what love is. I read that the other ...e bit where you try and fit the last bit in like when you ...e page and you got to the ...

056

Start a car pool

We think it was Keith Moon who drove a car into a pool. But that's not what we mean at all.

No. Let's be absolutely clear on that before we go any further.

What we're suggesting is that you help the environment and make life a bit friendlier by figuring out how to share lifts to and from work.

Liftshare.com is a website which helps people find drivers and passengers online.

Who knows. You might find some new friends while saving the planet. That's like helping two wounded birds with one bandage.

FYI: Every day 10 million seats go empty on the road.

057

Enjoy a Fairtrade brew

Fairtrade are the good guys. If they were in an old-fashioned cowboy movie, they'd be wearing white hats. If they were in a modern-day Arnold Schwarzenegger movie, they wouldn't be in the film at all, because it would be a bloody awful film. But maybe they'd be behind the camera – in fact they'd probably be doing the catering.

Because that's what they do, after all.

In the UK, we drink 31 billion cups of coffee every year.

And Fairtrade do other stuff. Like chocolate and bananas.

Mmmmmm.

Are you thinking what I'm thinking?

FYI: Keep an eye out when shopping for other eco-friendly labels such as the Marine Stewardship Association, Soil Association and anything Organic.

Guarantees a **better deal** for Third World Producers ®

FAIRTRADE

058

Pull the plug on mobile phone chargers

Your mobile phone charger is more powerful than it looks.

And 95% of the energy used by the phone chargers in this country is wasted. They're only doing their job – i.e. charging phones – for 5% of the time.

By comparison with this figure, the average 'it' girl is a crazed workaholic.

059

Praise people

'You're looking damned good today, CJ.'

'Great idea you had for the frozen fish client, Susan.'

'I'm so glad you're part of this meeting, Brian. You always make meetings come alive.'

That's the sort of thing. Now, practise sounding like you mean it. Because unfortunately in this country, praising someone else tends to sound like you're really a born-again Canadian who's won the Lottery and spent all the money going on motivational courses.

But it's worth persevering, because it makes everybody work better and it makes the workplace a whole lot happier.

For instance, I told the person who came up with this action how much I liked it.

They said how much they appreciated my views.

We both felt a little more grrrrrr than we had before.

060

Remember people's names

It's so much more courteous than going 'Hello, whatchamacallit. Have you met Buggerlugs?'

For tips on how to do this – which is kind of step one in office etiquette, if you think about it – go to mindtools.com.

I think that's the name of the site, anyway. It might be Frank or something beginning with L.

FYI:
Rhoshandiatellyneshiaunne veshenk Koyaanfsquatsiuty Williams is the proud owner of the longest name appearing on a birth certificate.

SCOTT

DOUG

061

Speak rather than email

It's nicer.

It's also better to see someone's reaction for real.

Plus, there's another reason. It's also because your boss can read all your emails.

Didn't you know this?

Why do you think he was looking at you so weirdly last Tuesday?

He KNOWS what you want to do with the office junior and a tub of low-fat yogurt.

Mark as unread

Out of office reply

Send

Receive

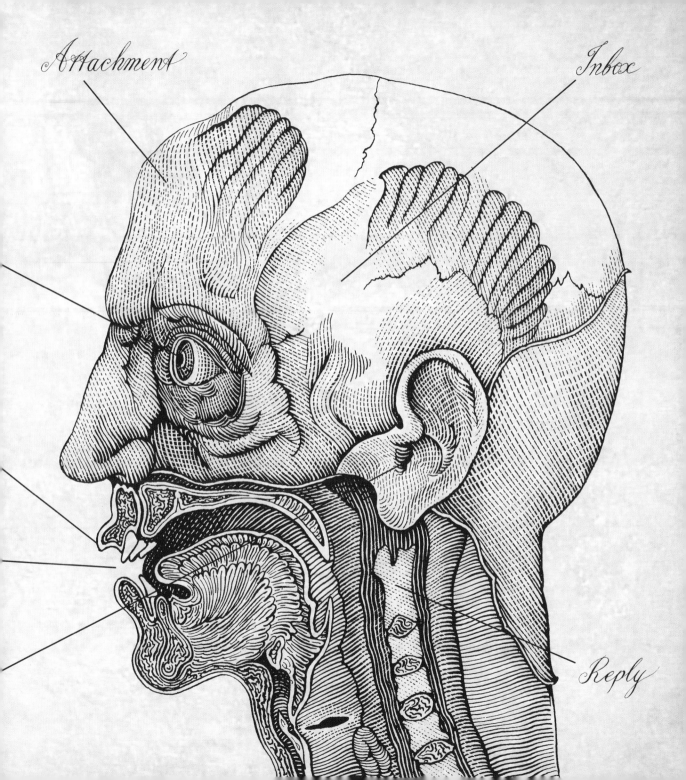

Attachment

Inbox

Reply

ACTION

062

Make a radio request for the person opposite you

Even if your workplace is
in Norwich and the DJ is
Alan Partridge.

A Guide To
Workplace Etiquette

Do greet your colleagues with a 'hello', or 'a jolly good morning to you' when entering your workplace.

Do laugh and smile. People rather like that.

Do say 'please' and 'thank you', please. Thank you.

Do tidy up after yourself. It's true what they say; tidy person, tidy mind and neat hair – usually.

Do try and avoid tardiness. Your meetings should always begin and end on time. It's oh so much nicer that way.

Do always try to listen. It's simply charming when people do.

Do remember people's birthdays. One day it will be yours.

Do try not to snoop into the business of others – no one likes a nosy parker.

Do compliment each other as often as possible. 'You make a lovely cup of tea' doesn't count.

Do pay your way at lunch. One should never underestimate how many people call you 'old tight wad', or worse.

063

Practise good manners

We don't stop being human beings just because we walk through that lobby where the receptionists sit in their glorious isolation, with the pot plant.

We're still human beings.

And human beings respond best to being treated with respect.

(In fact, if you're nice to someone, you can often get away with blue murder.)

It's the same with pot plants, spookily enough.

The only difference is that, with real people, it's best not to douse them with a watering can more than once a week.

064

Recycle your printer cartridges

We're serious. It's a lot easier than you'd think.

Go to actionaidrecycling.org.uk and you can find out all about it.

Of course, we wouldn't need printer cartridges at all, if those predictions from a few years back of 'the paper-free office', had come true.

Who was making those predictions?

Was it someone who was drunk?

Was it TV astrologer Russell Grant?

If so, Russell darling, you were clearly communicating via Uranus.

065

Pass this book around

As a business idea, this has to be one of the worst. But here we are, asking you to pass on this book to a friend, rather than telling said friend to fork out for it.

Why?

Because frankly there are more important things than the bottom line. ('Does my bottom line look big in this?') And we'd rather people shared things.

In fact, we like this idea so much that we're gonna give away pristine new copies of this book to anyone who can send theirs in, with signatures from 20 people who have read the book and then passed it on.

And anyone who thought – 'I could always cheat and forge 20 signatures' – well, honestly. Shame on you.

FYI: Find out how to exchange your old, well-thumbed book for a lovely, crisp new one at www.wearewhatwedo.org

Take breaks

Stress is infectious. If you get stressed out, you'll pass it on to someone else.

(Stress is like pass the parcel. Which is a pretty stressful game in itself. Especially if you work in MI5 security.)

So if you can avoid getting stressed out, you stop the vicious circle starting.

And the best way to do this is to take breaks.

You know all those books in the self-help section called things like 'Don't Sweat the Chicken Soup'?

We're gonna save you time and money now. They all tell you to – stop, take a deep breath, count to ten. Most times, you'll realise that the problem you're facing is something you've faced before or something that isn't gonna kill you this time.

Now you can bypass the self-help section completely.

FYI: The average British lunch 'hour' is now just 27 minutes.

067

Share your lunch with someone

That's it really. A simple, good idea.

As they say in the ads, it does exactly what it says on the tin.

Although if you are eating your lunch out of a tin, you may find a limited number of people willing to share it with you.

Cats, yes. People, less so.

068

Try a job swap

Everybody always thinks someone else has got a cushier job than them.

So why not try it?

Job swaps encourage empathy and bonding.

And they're surprisingly easy to organise.

I've got first bags on the guy who oils up the models on Hawaiian Tropic film shoots.

069

Shut down your computer properly

Yes, we know. It takes about 15 minutes, and it's as boring as listening to the weather forecast in Danish.

But it makes a huge difference.

If we all shut down our computers properly for a year, we'd undo all the damage that George Bush does in one typical morning.

Now, that may make you feel a bit defeatist.

(And frankly there's so much defeatism around, it just makes you want to give up.)

But we've got to start somewhere.

The journey of a thousand steps begins with pulling on your trainers and saying 'A thousand steps, huh? Is that like going to the station and back or is it longer than that?'

FYI: One computer left on all day results in the emission of 1,500 pounds of carbon dioxide in a year. It would take 100 to 500 trees to absorb that amount of extra carbon dioxide released into the atmosphere.

Turn off co

Save planet a bit

mputer

Save planet

Planet saved

Not bothered

070

Give as you go

Ask the people in finance about this.

Admit it – you've always wanted an excuse to go up and talk to that strangely attractive person who joined a few months ago.

Tell them you want to opt in to a payroll giving scheme.

If you do this, they're gonna be thinking: 1) you're a nice person, 2) you're good at maths, and 3) you're earning enough money to be able to be generous.

That's not a bad first impression.

Hell, I even fancy you a bit myself.

FYI: A monthly £10 payroll donation could cost as little as £6. See www.payrollgiving centre.org.uk

= £10

071

Practise mobile manners

We've all seen – and, worse, heard – the people who offend against this.

Probably most of us have been guilty of it ourselves – although maybe not to the extent shown here.

But the etiquette of using a mobile is pretty simple, really – just think of it as the opposite of great sex.

Keep it quiet.
And keep it short.

FYI: There are currently about 50 million mobile phones in use in the UK compared with around 25 million in 2000 and 4.5 million in 1995.

072

Lose the plastic cup

Plastic cups are the spawn of the devil.

Plastic cups are like a mixture of Chucky the ventriloquist's doll, the guy with the hockey mask and the Japanese girl on the black and white TV set.

When you next see a plastic cup at work, think about all this. If it makes you throw up with fear, maybe you've got an overactive imagination and you should cut down on the horror films for a bit.

But plastic cups are taking over the world and they're nasty.

FYI: Vending machines dispense 3 billion cups per year in the UK. A further 3 billion cups originate from other sources, and together these cups use 24,000 tonnes of polystyrene annually.

Photo: Nick Walker

Leave work on time at least once a week

When I see people leaving work bang on time, I think two things.

One, that person has got their priorities right. They'll probably live longer than me and have a happier life.

Two, they've got no chance in hell of being the next CEO.

But the fact is, we should all leave work on time – to spend time with our family.

We're not advocating leaving work early to spend time with Mr John Smith, Mr Johnny Walker and Ms Mirnoff Red in The Dog and Modem.

No. Just think of your family and stand up straight. Pack your things away and walk towards the door. If your boss stops you and says 'What the hell are you doing? It's only half past three', get a new watch.

But don't abandon the principle.

FYI: In the UK, we work the longest hours in Europe.

yipee

074

Turn away from your screen and...

If you look at your computer screen for too long, you become hypnotised.

How else can you explain the ridiculous behaviour of most people at work?

For instance, there are people who will tell you that they can't stand living in London. But they only live in London because that's where the high-paid work is, which allows them to pay the huge rents in London.

Plum stir crazy.

Until you realise that Paul McKenna is sitting inside each computer screen, hypnotising everybody.

And the biggest irony of all is this:
Paul lives in Borehamwood.

"I tried being nice to the temp"

075

Be nice to temps

Remember your first day at school?

It's like that for temps, the whole time.

Except that they're not wearing a uniform that doesn't fit and being asked questions about maths that mean nothing to them at all.

Unless your workplace is particularly weird, of course.

I worked in a place like that once.

076

Use one of these email signatures

If you don't know how to download them, go to our website and we'll show you.

If you don't know how to go to our website, ask someone in IT.

If you don't know how to turn your computer on, congratulations.

You must be the boss.

FYI: For instructions on how to set up email signatures, see wearewhatwedo.org

Try this:
Sorry this is an email and not a face-to-face conversation.

Or this:
If emails save time, not printing them saves trees.

Or this:
Be the change you want to see in the world.

Never, ever use stuff like this:
Character is forged in a crucible of adversity.

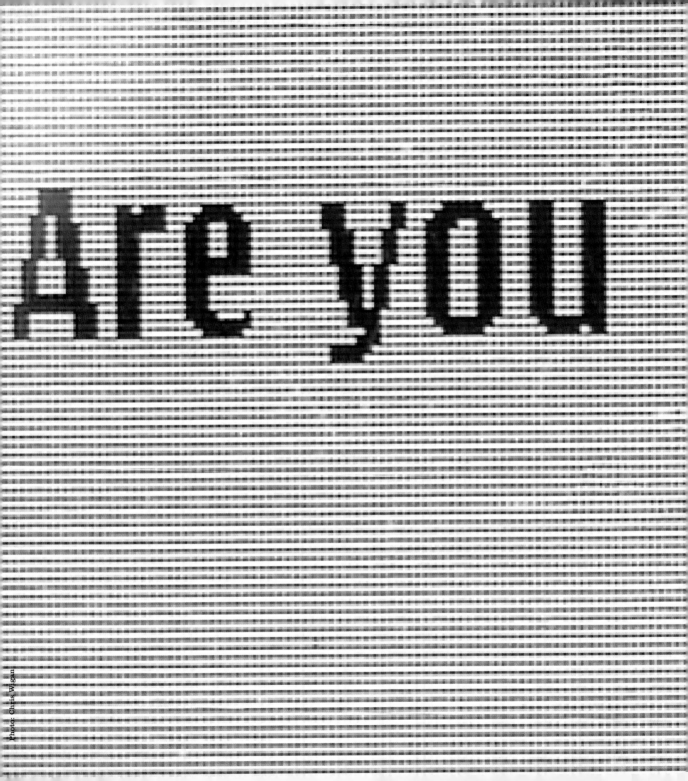

Are you

OK?

Show empathy

If you've ever had to go through a divorce while sitting in a meeting to discuss next year's sales figures, you'll find a new meaning to the words 'hell on earth'.

And every day, with measureless heroism, people are dealing with all kinds of terrible things.

So, even though each workplace has more soap stories than a Christmas double edition of 'TV Times', we're not asking you to stick your nose in where it's not wanted.

Just treat people with respect. Be aware that we are all sentient, suffering human beings.

FYI: An estimated 12 million people in the UK are on antidepressants.

078

Photocopy on both sides

How would you feel if your hairdresser only cut the hair on the left-hand side of your head?

How would you feel if Top Shop sold you a pair of trousers with only one leg?

How would you feel if you found out that Sven-Goran Eriksson had only been one-timing his lover?

There are two sides to every story – and two sides to every piece of paper.

FYI: The amount of waste paper buried in the UK each year would fill 103,448 double-decker buses.

079

Give up some spare time

You're probably thinking –
'Hang on a minute. What
spare time?'

But if you do the maths,
you'll realise that there are
whole spare hours in your life.

For instance, if you've got
time to watch Dick and Dom
on TV, play Freecell on your
computer, or read emails from
a supermarket – you've got
spare time.

If you ring up to take part
in Dick and Dom, play
Freecell and Minesweeper
to competition standard, or
write emails to supermarkets
– you have far, far too much
spare time.

If you used some of that
time to help other people,
you'd feel better.

It just happens to be one
of the few immutable laws of
the universe.

Choose your friends wisely

All businesses need to buy in services.

So, why not give your business to the ones who are more responsible and nicer people?

When you were at school, you hung around with people you liked – it was a concept called 'friendship' and it worked pretty well.

(Except when other concepts like 'who's the new girl?' and 'I saw her first' briefly entered the picture.)

But imagine a day, in the not too distant future, when all business is done like that. Where business is built on friendship, respect and trust.

FYI: When making a purchasing decision 82 per cent of us believe it is important that the supplier shows a high degree of social responsibility.

081

Challenge your business about its 'lights on at night' policy

Stride into your boss's office.

Stare hard and say 'The trouble with you is that the lights are on, but there's nobody at home.'

Other good insults are to say 'The lift doesn't go to the top floor, does it?' Or 'You're having a blonde moment, aren't you?', or 'You must have been born in the stupid tree and hit every branch on the way down.'

The last three are just gratuitous insults – and only to be used if you've just won the Lottery.

But the first one has a serious point to it.

After all, just what is the point in leaving lights on when there's nobody there?

FYI: Turning off unnecessary electric lights would reduce the average company's energy bill by up to 19%. Turn the lights off and read the page opposite.

Photo: Nick Walker

082

'Aspire not have more, be more.'

Archbishop Oscar Romero

Known as the Bishop of the Poor for his passionate defence of poor farmers' rights in El Salvador and for his courageous opposition to the genocide, Oscar Romero died for his beliefs at the hands of an unknown assassin in 1980.

to
but to

Learn to save a life

Nuff said.

THE ABC OF CPR.

The recovery position ensures that an unconscious person maintains an open airway, that the tongue cannot be swallowed, and that any vomit or fluid will not cause choking.

Ensure the person is lying on their side, supported by one leg and one arm.

Keep the airway open by tilting their head and lifting the chin.

If the airway is not open and the person is not breathing, begin resuscitation ABC.

A – airway
B – breathing
C – circulation

FYI: CPR = cardiopulmonary resuscitation. It's strongly recommended that you learn how to do it by taking a course. See www.redcross.org.uk

Airway

To open the airway, lift the chin with one hand, while pushing down on the forehead with the other to tilt the head back. Once the airway is open, look for chest movement and listen and feel for breathing by placing an ear close to the person's mouth.

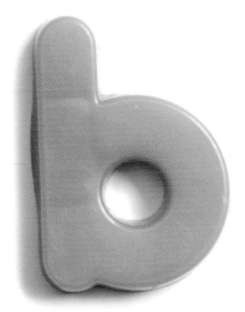

Breathing

If opening the airway does not cause the person to begin to breathe spontaneously, artificial respiration must be started.

Tilt their head back, lift up the chin, and pinch the nostrils together.

Take a deep breath and seal your mouth over the other person's mouth.

Breathe slowly into the person's mouth, and check that their chest rises.

Repeat until the person starts breathing or until assistance arrives.

Circulation

If there is no heart beat and no pulse (i.e. no circulation) and if no trained medical help is available, start 'external chest compression'.

Place the heel of one hand on the middle of the person's breastbone, and the heel of the other hand on top of the first. Lock the fingers and keep them off their chest.

Keeping elbows straight, press downwards firmly and quickly with hands then relax and repeat compression. Press down approximately 2 inches. The rate of compression should be approximately 100 compressions per minute. Do 15 compressions, and then give artificial respiration twice. Then repeat until assistance arrives.

084

Smile when you answer the phone

You can hear a smile.

And we don't mean that in any kind of hippy 'I can sing a rainbow' kind of way.

Let alone some kind of drugged-out 'I can smell spiders coming out of my sandwich' sort of way.

It's just one of those common-sense, makes-the-world-better, makes-business-better kind of things.

Of course you might be one of those people who think work should be terribly SERIOUS.

But it's worth remembering that people like that generally provide the most laughs for everybody else.

085

Support small businesses

Use your local newsagent, your local cab company, and your local local.

At the rate we're going, it's been calculated that all small businesses will have disappeared in 10 years.

Leaving the world run by Tesco.

Now, doubtless the world run by Tesco would be a lovely place – with all the trees arranged in themed aisles, a pervasive smell of freshly-baked croissants and lots of chocolate in the funeral parlours. (Or check-out zones, as they'd become known.)

But we'd miss corner shops when they were gone.

FYI: There are 3.7 million businesses in the UK, and 99% of these have fewer than 50 employees.

086

Avoid waste

OK, this sounds like a boring, worthy bit of advice.

And maybe it is.

Someone has calculated that if everyone in UK offices saved one staple a day, that would be 120 tonnes of metal saved a year.

As the old blues song nearly had it, '120 tonnes and what do you get? Another day older and deeper in debt.'

I can't take staples very seriously, to be honest. But the person who worked out that calculation takes all this stuff very seriously.

And if they've gone to all that trouble, the least you can do is think about it.

I mean, look at this staple-free stapled page. It's pretty cool, isn't it?

FYI: This page has been stapled with a Stapless Stapler.

BINGO

24/7	At the end of the day	Benchmark	Best practice	Bottom line
Walk the walk	Critical path	Game plan	Road map	Join the dots
In the loop	Brain dump	Level playing field	No-brainer	FYI
Outside the box	Push the envelope	Reinventing the wheel	Shoot from the hip	Singing from the same song sheet
Touch base	User-friendly	Value added	Keep me in the loop	Win-win

087

Play bullshit bingo

Tick off anything you hear in a meeting. First to complete a line wins.

What is this doing in a book like this? It's here because we believe jargon isn't just ugly, it's exclusive and power-based.

It's one of the things that makes working inhuman and joyless.

If you complete a whole card in one meeting, you can take your boss to the European Court of Human Rights. Plus, you win a toaster and a huge fluffy orange rabbit.

088

Get off one stop early

Legend tells of the great celluloid cowboy John Wayne turning to one of his younger cowpoke friends and uttering the immortal words 'Get off your horse and drink your milk.' (From the film 'There's Rustlers in Them Thar Hills, You Mark My Words, Mister.')

But we'd all be a lot healthier if we got off our trains or buses earlier and walked instead.

Thirty minutes walking per day cuts the risk of heart disease by half. It'll clear your brain as well. Blow the cobwebs away.

As my old mum used to say.

As she lay on the sofa, six inches deep in dust, drinking a four-pack of Guinness.

FYI: Each person in the UK walks over 50 miles less per year than 15 years ago.

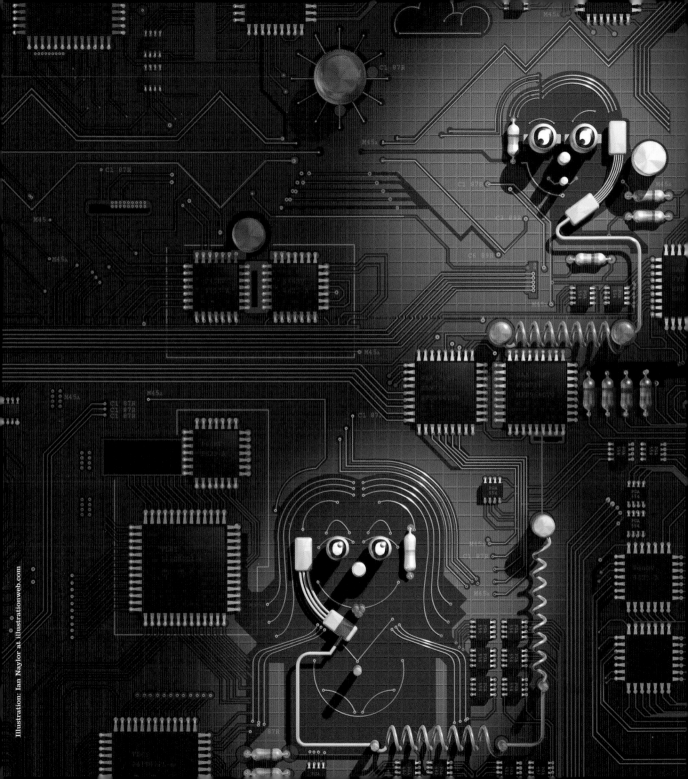

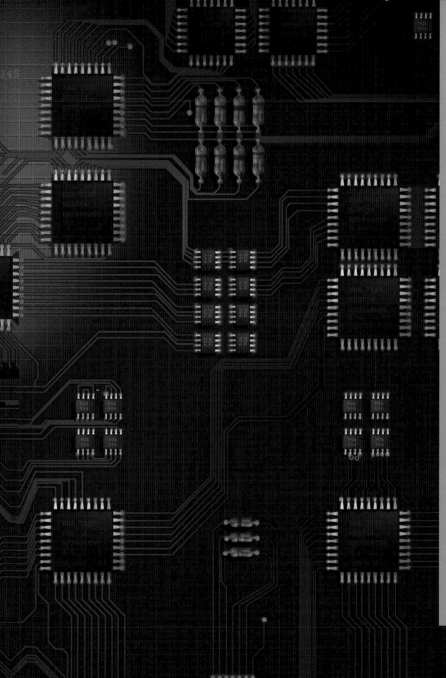

089

Ring the IT help desk just to see how they are

Are the people who work in IT human beings?

To answer that question, you first need to ask this – will they work better if you just turn them off and start them up again? After all, that's how the people in IT respond when your machine doesn't work.

(The technical term is 'rebooting'. As in 'if this machine doesn't work soon, I'm going to reboot it out the window.')

But the people who man the IT desk aren't machines.

And in fact, there are nearly a million real people in this country working in the IT industry.

So, try getting on with them before they take over completely.

090

Send this to your boss

In 2002, the Industrial Society found that 65% of businesses would change their policies if pushed by employees.

Give it a go.

Dear _____

When I was young I dreamt of being a *rock star / model / Premier League footballer / footballer's wife / _____ .

Next I thought about *scientist / entrepreneur / actor / reality TV star / _____ .

Now I am here: (department name) _____
(job title) _____ (extension) _____ .

In case you can't place me, I'm the one with (brief physical description) _____
_____ .

I still have a dream but it isn't just about me any more. Its about us at (organisation's name) _____ , and the difference we could make in the world.

I dream of working for an organisation that thinks about what we're doing to the planet and those around us and considers how we could do things better.

I dream of working for a manager who doesn't just think about people as numbers on a spreadsheet but who understands that we're each individuals and that we give of our best when we are valued.

But most of all, I dream of working with people who share my dreams.

Do you have time for a sandwich one lunchtime?

Yours sincerely

_____

* delete as appropriate

091

Take the stairs

Now, I could worry you with lots of stories about lifts that go wrong. The lift in our building, for instance, is made by a company called Schindler. Schindler's Lift. True story.

Not just about Schindler in wartime Germany. It's a true story that our lift is made by a company called Schindler.

And lifts go wrong.

If you've ever imagined being stuck in an upright box with eight halitotic colleagues, it's like doing the Christmas party stone cold sober.

So take the stairs. It cuts down your chances of heart disease, osteoporosis and diabetes.

Plus, if halitosis is catching, you're less likely to catch that as well.

FYI: Climb Everest without leaving the office – use stairs and a download to help you work this out www.wearewhatwedo.org/everest

092

Bring your kids into work for the day

It's very interesting what happens when you do this. People suddenly look more human.

They lose a little of that stiffness and starchiness.

Partly because it's not easy to look serious when you've got projectile vomit on your shoulder – and instead of last quarter's sales figures, you're carrying Benjamin Bunny.

Really accomplished players can try this – have a trans-atlantic video conferencing call while changing the nappy on one of those dolls that wets itself.

You know, the ones that **tell you** they've wet themselves.

093

Don't judge someone by the job they do

For instance: just because someone is a corporate lawyer, doesn't mean that they are necessarily a selfish, heartless person driven by greed.

Honestly, it doesn't.

No – honestly, honestly, honestly – it really doesn't.

It doesn't.

Ok, 99 times out 100, it does. But keep believing and you'll meet the 100th one day.

EU Presentation

SUMMIT MEETING

FINISH NOVEL

Company Report

Holiday accounts

Dissertation

BOILER

IN

094

Make a coffee for someone busier than you

If we all did this, the workplace would feel like it was all pulling together.

There would be a happier environment, and almost certainly greater productivity as a side effect.

Plus, the workaholics in the place would be twitching and gibbering from caffeine over-stimulation.

So, no change there.

095

Earn fewer air miles

Tough one, this. Cheap air travel is, let's face it, a nice thing.

So, asking you to cut back on it sounds like the killjoy equivalent to someone saying 'cut back on music' or 'cut back on sex'.

But, just for a minute, look at the facts – air travel is the fastest growing contributor to climate change, spewing nearly ten times more CO_2 into the sky than an equivalent train journey.

Or 100% more CO_2 than not travelling at all and opting for a video conference call once in a while.

Come on – video conferencing isn't that bad.

That jerky movement and time delay on the sound makes everyone look like they're in a 1970's Thunderbirds episode.

Enjoy it.

FYI: Flying from London to Edinburgh produces 193kg of CO_2, eight times the 23.8kg produced by taking the train. Moreover, the pollution is released at an altitude where its effect on climate change is more than double that on the ground.

if...

if I'd seen you weren't eating

if I'd noticed that you couldn't cope

if I'd known you woke up every night crying

if I'd thought you didn't get the joke

if I'd thought.

096

Blow the whistle on workplace bullies

1 in 3 employees say they've been bullied at work.

097

Say thanks

'Thank you.'

They're quite possibly the nicest two words in the language.

Because, like praise, gratitude is its own virtue. It just works.

You know when you get a note or even an email saying 'thank you'?

How does it make you feel?

I always think they've sent it to the wrong person. (And usually they have.)

But it's nice nonetheless.

And there's another nice word – 'nonetheless'.

FYI: 100% of Britons would feel more appreciated if they were thanked.

Spread
the word

There are three advantages
in going to the toilet.

One, is fairly obvious.
It stops us making a frankly
rather embarrassing mess in
our workspace.

Two, it's got a mirror; so we
can check that we're still the
drop-dead killer-gorgeous
people who left home that
morning.

And three, it gives us time
to think.

We all need time on our own,
when people can't get at us.
Sanctuary time, you could
call it.

Or 'popping to the loo', you
could call it.

So, why not stick up this
poster in your work toilet?

It'll give people something
positive to think about –
between doing numbers 1
and 2 above.

'We must be the change
we want to see in the world'
Mahatma Gandhi

099

Know how you fit into the bigger picture

Serious one, this.

When John Kennedy bumped into a janitor at NASA and asked him what he did, the man replied 'helping to put a man on the moon'.

That's a genuinely inspiring story.

And it raises the question: how many of us really understand the vision behind what we do in our working lives?

Incidentally, when the janitor asked Kennedy what HE was doing there, Kennedy apologised and admitted he'd walked into the ladies toilet by mistake.

100

Fail

It was Thomas Edison who said he invented the lightbulb because he'd previously invented 99 things that weren't a lightbulb.

It was Oscar Wilde who said genius was 1% inspiration and 99% perspiration.

And it was someone else whose name escapes me who said 'We learn more from our mistakes than from our successes'.

All true. Businesses make a cult of success, but the most successful people in the long run are the ones who aren't afraid to fail.

Talking of which, here are some ideas which didn't make it into the book.

I look on them all very fondly.

It's rather like our friends – usually, we like them more because of their failings.

Illustration: Sarah Carr

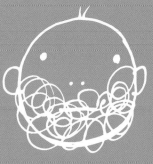

GROW A BEARD...
YOU CAN GET OUT
OF BED LATER.

SUPPORT
NATIONAL DOUGHNUT DAY.

Get a plant. They're
good for hiding behind.

Play practical jokes.

Have 'fancy-dress' Fridays once a month.

SING OUT LOUD AT LEAST ONCE A DAY.

REDUCE HEATING BILLS. WEAR A JUMPER.

PUT DISCO-BALLS IN THE LIGHT FIXTURES.

Find out more:

Carbon footprint	www.carbonfootprint.com	www.bp.com//
	www.earthday.net	www.climatecare.org
Carbon neutral	www.co2balance.com	www.flightpledge.org.uk
	www.carbonneutral.com	www.treesforcities.org
Clothing	www.howies.co.uk	www.saftag.com
Fairtrade	www.clipper-teas.com	www.cafedirect.co.uk
	www.fairtrade.org.uk	www.fairtrade.ie
	www.co-op.co.uk	www.yorkshiretea.co.uk
	www.walesfairtradeforum.org.uk	www.leafshop.co.uk
Green energy	www.good-energy.co.uk	www.greenenergy.uk.com
	www.ecotricity.co.uk	www.foe.co.uk
	www.mwea.org.uk	www.ecocentre.org.uk
	www.renewscotland.org	www.foe-scotland.org.uk
Green resources	www.letsrecycle.com	www.freecycle.org
	www.inkinddirect.org	www.computer-aid.org
	www.paper-round.co.uk	www.recycle-more.co.uk
	www.recyclenow.com	www.save-a-cup.co.uk
	www.raceagainstwaste.ie	www.pcb-plus.co.uk
	www.envocare.co.uk	www.wastewatch.org.uk
	www.wasteonline.org.uk	www.scotlink.org
	www.wascot.org.uk	www.climate-concern.com
	www.thecarbontrust.co.uk	www.consultnet.ie
	www.est.org.uk	www.cylch.org
	www.wasteawarenesswales.org.uk	www.walesenvtrust.org.uk
	www.greenconsumerguide.com	www.rainforest-alliance.org
	www.mpsonline.org.uk/mpsr (stop junk mail)	
Cartridge recycling	www.recyclingappeal.com	www.actionaidrecycling.org.uk
	www.childrenshospital.ie	www.collect4school.co.uk
Office supplies	www.goodnessdirect.co.uk	www.we-are-one.org.uk
	www.belu.org	www.divinechocolate.com
	www.innocentdrinks.co.uk	www.naturalcollection.com
	www.greenstat.co.uk	www.remarkable.co.uk
	www.recycledproducts.org.uk	www.ecoprint.org.uk
	www.ecover.com	
Organic food	www.soilassociation.org	www.organicfood.co.uk
	www.abel-cole.co.uk	www.localfoodworks.org
	www.soilassociationscotland.org	www.organicwales.com
	www.eattheseasons.co.uk	www.msc.org
Payroll giving	www.givingcampaign.org.uk	www.bitc.org.uk
	www.allaboutgiving.org	www.payrollgivingcentre.org.uk
Training provider	www.equalitytraining.co.uk	
Recruitment	www.prospect-us.co.uk	
Small business information	www.smallbusiness.co.uk	www.fsb.org.uk
	www.plato.ie	
Travel	www.eta.co.uk	www.tourismconcern.org.uk
	www.responsibletravel.com	www.northsouthtravel.co.uk
	www.travelroots.com	www.shareacar.com
	www.liftshare.com	www.carclubs.org.uk
	www.carsharewales.com	www.flightpledge.org.uk
Volunteering	www.employeevolunteering.org.uk	www.timebank.org.uk
	www.volunteer.ie	www.do-it.org.uk
	www.bbc.co.uk	www.ncvo-vol.org.uk
	www.volunteering.org.uk	www.volunteering-wales.net
	www.horsesmouth.co.uk	www.volunteerscotland.info
Health and wellbeing	www.doh.gov.uk	www.irishhealth.ie
	www.optometrists.ie	www.everydaysport.com
	www.redcross.org.uk	www.redcross.ie
	www.employersforwork-lifebalance.org.uk	www.stjohnwales.org.uk
Workplace bullying	www.tuc.org.uk	www.workplacebullying.co.uk

Please visit www.wearewhatwedo.org for all current websites/resources
We Are What We Do does not receive money from any websites mentioned in this book and is not responsible for their content.

Things to do, boxes to tick: ✓

51 Find out where your lunch has come from
52 Recycle waste paper
53 Calculate your carbon footprint
54 Don't be an ideas killer
55 Use a biro from start to finish
56 Start a car pool
57 Enjoy a Fairtrade brew
58 Pull the plug on mobile phone chargers
59 Praise people
60 Remember people's names
61 Speak rather than email
62 Make a radio request for the person opposite you
63 Practise good manners
64 Recycle your printer cartridges
65 Pass this book around
66 Take breaks
67 Share your lunch with someone
68 Try a job swap
69 Shut down your computer properly
70 Give as you go
71 Practise mobile manners
72 Lose the plastic cup
73 Leave work on time at least once a week
74 Turn away from your screen and... blink
75 Be nice to temps
76 Use one of these email signatures
77 Show empathy
78 Photocopy on both sides
79 Give up some spare time
80 Choose your friends wisely
81 Challenge your business about its 'lights on at night' policy
82 Aspire not to have more, but to be more
83 Learn to save a life
84 Smile when you answer the phone
85 Support small businesses
86 Avoid waste
87 Play bullshit bingo
88 Get off one stop early
89 Ring the IT help desk just to see how they are
90 Send this to your boss
91 Take the stairs
92 Bring your kids into work for the day
93 Don't judge someone by the job they do
94 Make a coffee for someone busier than you
95 Earn fewer air miles
96 Blow the whistle on workplace bullies
97 Say thanks
98 Spread the word
99 Know how you fit into the bigger picture
100 Fail

We would not have been able to print this book without the following companies agreeing to place advance orders:

1 BDO Stoy Hayward
2 ICI
3 Abbey
4 Antidote
5 Corporate Research Forum
6 David Abbott & Partners
7 YSC
8 Financial Services Authority
9 Good Business
10 Marks & Spencer
11 O2
12 Tate & Lyle
13 Ben and Jerry's
14 Credit Suisse
15 Herbert Smith LLP
16 horsesmouth.co.uk
17 Barclays
18 BAA
19 Coca-Cola Great Britain
20 Emap plc
21 Ethical Corporation
22 Kingfisher plc
23 3UK
24 Accenture
25 HSBC
26 Lehman Brothers
27 Lyndales
28 Samsung Electronics
29 The Daily Telegraph
30 Shell
31 Tayburn
32 Wieden + Kennedy
33 Autobytel
34 Sainsbury's
35 Trinity Management Communications
36 ProspectUs
37 Design X
38 Business in the Community
39 JWT – part of WPP plc

We Are What We Do:

Alison Howard
Andy Burgess
Becca Leed
Christian Strasser
David Robinson
Eliza Anderson (Australia)
Eugénie Harvey
Fiona Wollensack
(Germany/Austria/Switzerland)

Frances Clarke
Jamie Pourier
Kenn Jordan
Linda Woolston
Lycia Harper
Michael Enright
Nick Walker
Patricia Taterra
(Germany/Austria/Switzerland)

Paul Edney
(Canada/USA)
Roger Granada
(Spain/South America)
Sandra Deeble
Sara Smith-Laing
Stanley Harris
Steve Wish
Tanis Taylor

Many individuals and organisations have contributed to the creation of this book.

We would especially like to thank the following:

Illustration Ltd for working with their illustrators to create these images. In particular, we would like to thank Juliette Lott for coordination.

The Book Service (part of the Random House Group) for providing storage and distribution, especially Richard Hoban.

Good Business and **Business in the Community** for unflinching support throughout the development of the project and in particular Gail Greengross (BITC) and Giles Gibbons (Good Business).

JWT for re-touching and photographic locations.

Wieden + Kennedy for creative support throughout the development of We Are What We Do.

Brunswick Group for providing We Are What We Do with free office space.

Short Books and **Faber & Faber** for on-going support.

Tom Long and the team at Coca-Cola Great Britain, whose early support for our vision got the ball rolling.

BDO Stoy Hayward for help with promotion across the UK.

And finally, we'd like to acknowledge the tremendous support of **Sainsbury's** with both 'Change the World for a Fiver' and 'Change the World 9 to 5'.

Allen & Overy LLP
Antidote
ArthurSteeneHorneAdamson
BITC Ireland
BITC Northern Ireland
Community Links
Create-a-Net
Eden Project Books/Guardian Books
Framfab
Good Business
Hardie Grant Publishing
Interbrand
International Literary Agency
Joffe Charitable Trust
Lincoln Centre
Lyndales Solicitors
New Society Publishers
Pendo Verlag
Pilotlight Australia
Precise Media
Timberland Boot Company
TimeBank

Alan Parker
Alessandra Lariu
Anne Shewring
Annie Taylor
Aurea Carpenter
Barbara Crowther
Ben Wish
Bill Greenhead
Brendan May
Briony Greenhill
Caroline Church
Chris Pease
Caroline Peat
Chris Winn
Christina Hemming
Colin Elgie
Conrad Gutekunst
David Cameron
Deborah Keay
Ellie Robinson
Fiona Hague
Francesca Fairbairn
Gemma McNeilis
Giles Gibbons
Gordon Brown
Gracie Ashton
Gray Joliffe
Helen Fuchs
Ian Baker
Ian Naylor
Jane Tewson
Katie Carruthers
Kathleen Murphy
Kay Harper
Kevin King
Larissa Howard
Leo Hickman
Linda Bronson
Lisa Hall
Lisa Nice
Liz Mills
Louise Ellison
Lucinda Frostick
Michael Jacobs
Nicki Kennedy
Niki Bowers
Paul Twivy
Peter Davies
Philip Murphy
Ray Eckerman
Rebecca Hastings
Rebecca Nicolson
Richard Harries
Richard Mason
Richard McKeever
Richard Phipps
Rod Hunt
Roger Granada
Rosanna Walker
Sam Edenborough
Sandra Deeble
Sholto Walker
Struan Wallace
Tanis Taylor
Tim Reith

we are what we do©